Contents

KU-663-091

Any words appearing in bold, **like this**, are explained in the Glossary.

About the experiments and demonstrations

This book contains some boxes headed 'Science Answers'. Each one describes an experiment or demonstration that you can try yourself. In doing them you will get a chance to understand how your body works, or how it responds to different situations.

Materials you will use

Most of the experiments and demonstrations in this book can be done with objects that you can find in your own home. You will also need a pencil and paper to record your results.

How does my body work?

Your body is like an incredibly clever machine. It has many different parts and each part has its own job to do. All the parts work together perfectly, so your body can do many different jobs at the same time. You can use your body to do a huge range of things, such as kicking a ball, reading a book, or eating an apple. But this is not all your body can do. It also works all the time to keep you alive.

Every second of the day and night, your body is busy. Your lungs are taking in air and pushing it out again, your heart is pumping blood around your body, and your **digestive system** is breaking down your food. All these activities are **automatic** – which means you don't ever have to think about making them happen.

What can I learn about my body?

In this book you can find out more about how your body works. You can learn what happens when you move, breathe and eat, and find out how your blood is pumped round your body. You can also discover how you grow and how you use your **senses** to help you to see, hear, feel, taste and smell things.

What is my body made from?

Your body is made up of billions of tiny **cells**. They are so small that they can only be seen under a very powerful microscope. Cells are the building blocks from which everything in your body is made. There are hundreds of different kinds of body cells and each type does a different job. They join together to make all the parts of your body – your bones, muscles and blood and all your **organs**, such as your heart and brain.

What does my body look like inside?

Inside your body there are bones, muscles, blood vessels and organs, and all of them are made from millions of cells. The cells of an organ, such as the brain, are very different from the cells of your bones or blood.

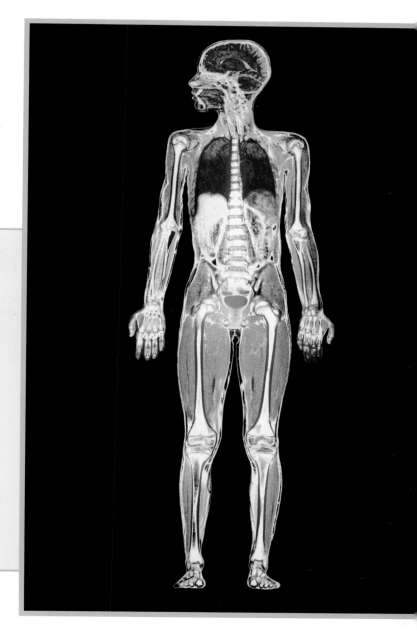

How do I move and grow?

Inside your body there are hundreds of muscles and bones that work together to keep you moving. Your bones provide a strong **framework** for all your body parts, and your muscles pull on your bones to make this framework move.

What do my bones do?

There are more than 200 bones in your body, and they all link together to make your skeleton. Your skeleton gives your body its shape and keeps you upright. It also protects your internal **organs**. For example, your brain is covered by your skull, and your heart and lungs are kept safe inside your ribs. Your skeleton is much more than just a rigid frame – it can also bend and **swivel** in many different directions. All the bones in your body are linked by **joints** and most of these joints are moveable. Moveable joints allow your bones to move in many directions. You can find out more about how joints work on page 10.

What's inside my bones?

This is what your thigh bone looks like inside. Your bones have a hard outer layer of solid bone and a slightly softer inner layer, called spongy bone. In the centre is a space filled with jelly-like **bone marrow**. Your bone marrow makes new blood **cells**. Bones need blood to supply them with food and **oxygen**. **Blood vessels** deliver blood to the spongy bone. A substance called **cartilage** covers the end of the bone at your hip joint.

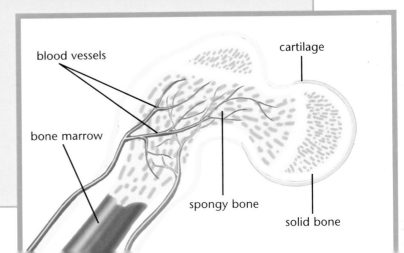

blood vessels

cartilage

bone marrow

spongy bone

solid bone

What are the parts of the human skeleton?

This picture shows the main bones in your body. Every bone has a scientific name and some have everyday names as well. For example, the sternum is usually known as the breastbone.

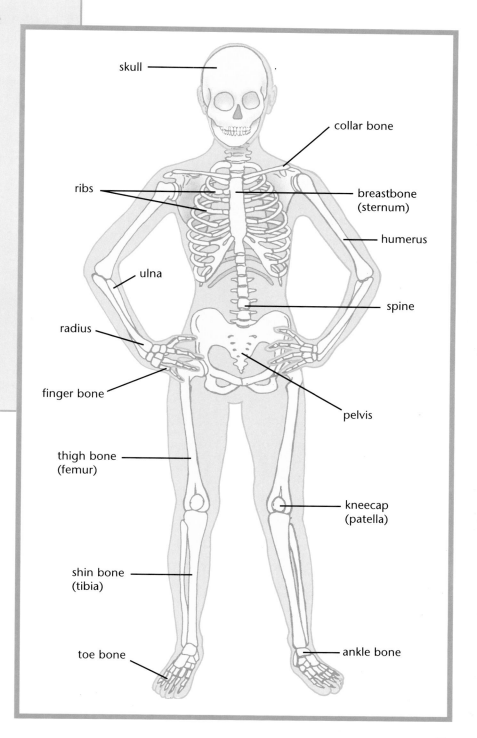

skull

collar bone

ribs

breastbone (sternum)

humerus

ulna

radius

spine

finger bone

pelvis

thigh bone (femur)

kneecap (patella)

shin bone (tibia)

toe bone

ankle bone

What do my muscles do?

Muscles are responsible for every movement you make – from blinking and breathing to jumping and swallowing. Many of your muscles are attached to bones. These muscles pull on your bones to make your joints move. But not all muscles work with bones. There are muscles in the walls of your heart that push your blood round your body, and muscles in your **intestines** that squeeze your food through your **digestive system**. These muscle movements happen **automatically** inside your body and cannot be seen at all from the outside.

Face muscles

You have over 40 muscles in your face – more than any other animal. This means you can make an incredibly wide range of expressions.

8

How do muscles work?

Muscles can make two movements – they can **contract** (tighten and shorten) and they can **relax** (loosen and lengthen). Muscles sometimes work in pairs, so one contracts while the other relaxes. When muscles are attached to bones, one muscle in the pair pulls the bone one way, then the other muscle pulls the bone back again.

Muscles at work

This diagram shows how the muscles in your upper arm work together. You can feel a pair of muscles at work in your upper arm. When you raise your fist to your shoulder, the muscles in the front of your arm – called your biceps – contract, getting shorter and fatter, to pull up your arm. At the same time, the muscles in the back of your arm – your triceps – relax and lengthen. When you bring your fist down, your triceps contract to pull your arm straight and your biceps relax.

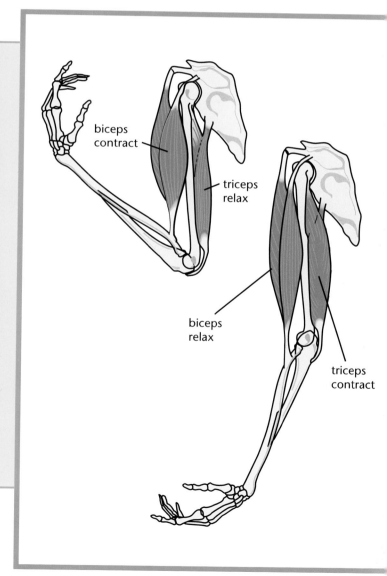

biceps
contract

triceps
relax

biceps
relax

triceps
contract

How do joints work?

In order to move around, you need muscles, bones and joints. It would be no good trying to move your bones if they didn't have joints to allow them to bend. There are several different types of joints in your body. Your elbow and knee are hinge joints. They work like hinges on a door to allow your lower arm and leg to swing backwards and forwards.

Why can the shoulder joint swivel?

Your shoulder and hip are ball-and-socket joints (see diagram of hip joint on page 11). The bone in your upper arm ends in a ball, which fits into a cup-like socket in your shoulder bone. The ball swivels in its socket, allowing your arm to move in many directions.

What does a joint look like?

In a moveable joint, the ends of the bones are covered by a **flexible** substance called cartilage. Cartilage is smooth and slippery and allows the bones to glide over each other. The two bone tips are held together by tough, stretchy straps called **ligaments**. Inside the space formed by the ligaments is some fluid that helps the bones glide more smoothly.

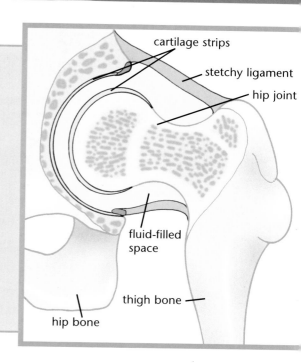

cartilage strips

stetchy ligament

hip joint

fluid-filled space

thigh bone

hip bone

How do I grow taller?

As children get older, some of their bones become longer, making them taller. The bones that grow most are your leg bones. Near the ends of each growing bone are bands made from cartilage. The cells in these bands **multiply** to grow new cartilage, making the bone gradually longer. By the time you are 25, your cartilage cells stop multiplying and you stop growing.

How do babies develop and grow?

Your body grows and changes throughout your childhood, but it grows fastest of all before you are born. The process begins when two single cells from the mother and the father join together to form an embryo – a **microscopic** ball of cells that will develop into a baby. During the first few weeks of pregnancy the cells in the embryo multiply into hundreds and then thousands and then millions. As this happens, the ball of cells grows and changes shape. After two months it is a tiny baby, the size of a thumb. It already has a heart and many other body parts. By nine months, the baby is fully developed and ready to live outside its mother's body.

What is blood for?

In order to work, the **cells** in your body need **oxygen**, food and other **chemicals**. It is your blood that supplies you with these things. Blood is your body's transport system. It travels all round your body, delivering all the things your cells need and taking away any waste.

How does blood travel round my body?

Your blood travels all round your body in a vast network of tubes called **blood vessels**. At the centre of this network is your heart, which is working constantly to make your blood **circulate** around your body. Together, your heart, blood vessels and blood are known as the circulation system.

The blood vessels that carry blood away from the heart are called **arteries**. The ones bringing blood to the heart are called **veins**. Your arteries and veins divide many times, becoming smaller and smaller until they form tiny blood vessels called **capillaries**. The capillaries that lead from your arteries join up with the capillaries leading from your veins to create a complete network, so your blood can travel all the way around your body.

What happens to my blood?

When your heart beats, blood is pushed into your arteries, and then through smaller and smaller blood vessels until it reaches your capillaries. Capillaries are so small they can reach right in between your body cells. As blood flows along a capillary, oxygen, food and other chemicals pass through the capillary walls into the surrounding cells. At the same time, waste products from your cells (such as **carbon dioxide**, see page 17) pass into your blood.

After the blood has made its deliveries, it continues travelling through larger and larger blood vessels into your veins. Then it arrives back at your heart. But before it starts its journey round the body again it visits the lungs, where it picks up oxygen and drops off waste products.

How does the circulation system work?

Your heart, blood vessels and blood are known as the circulation system. This diagram shows how your circulation system works. The arteries (red) carry blood with dissolved oxygen away from the heart to the rest of the body. The veins (blue) bring blood that has lost its oxygen back to the heart.

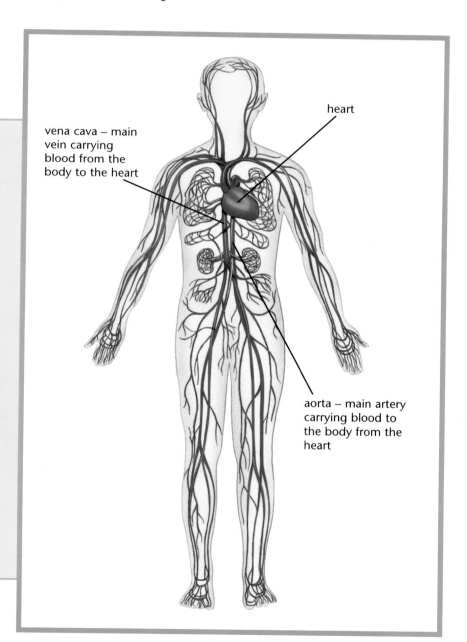

heart

vena cava – main vein carrying blood from the body to the heart

aorta – main artery carrying blood to the body from the heart

What does my heart do?

Your heart is a hollow ball of muscle that pushes your blood around your body. It beats about 100,000 times a day without getting tired! Your heart is divided into two halves, and each half has two chambers (or sections) – an upper chamber, called an atrium, and a lower chamber, called a ventricle. In between the chambers are flaps that act like one-way doors, making sure your blood flows the right way.

Blood from the main veins of your body flows into the atria (upper chambers). When the atria are filled with blood their muscular walls **contract** and squeeze blood into the ventricles. Once the ventricles have filled up with blood, it is their turn to contract and push blood into the main arteries of the body.

What does it look like inside your heart?

This diagram shows the main parts of your heart. The right side takes in blood from your body and sends it to your lungs. The left side takes in blood from your lungs and pumps it round the rest of your body.

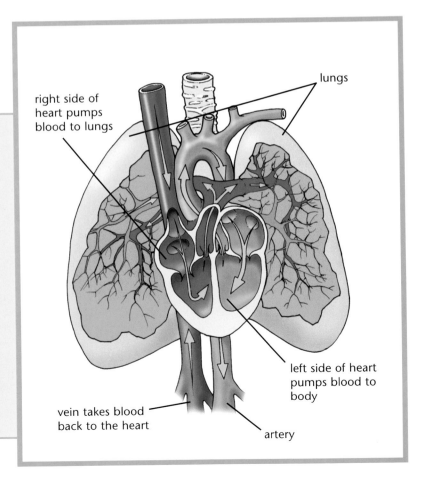

right side of heart pumps blood to lungs

lungs

left side of heart pumps blood to body

vein takes blood back to the heart

artery

EXPERIMENT: Does your heartbeat change after exercise?

HYPOTHESIS:
Exercise makes your heart beat faster.

EQUIPMENT:
A watch that counts seconds.

EXPERIMENT STEPS:

1 Lay the first two or three fingers of your right hand over the wrist of your left hand, so that your fingertips cover the area below the thumb. You should be able to feel the regular beat of your blood being pumped through your veins. This is called your **pulse**.

2 When you have found your pulse, count the number of beats in 20 seconds.

3 Jump up and down on the spot for a few minutes until you are hot and out of breath.

4 Now take your pulse again, counting the number of beats in 20 seconds. Is the number different from before?

5 Write down what you found.

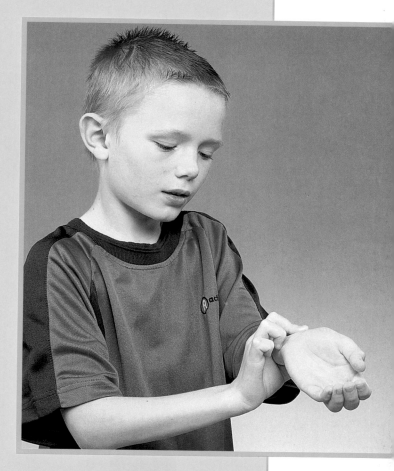

CONCLUSION:
Your heart beats faster after exercise, because when your body is using more energy it needs more blood delivered to it fast.

Why do I breathe?

Your body **cells** need **oxygen** to help them get energy from food. Oxygen is an invisible gas in the air. When you breathe in oxygen, it travels deep into your lungs, where it is absorbed by your blood and taken to all your body cells.

What happens when I breathe?

The parts of your body that you use for breathing are called your respiratory system. They include your nose and mouth, your throat, your windpipe (or trachea) and the two spongy lungs in your chest. When you breathe in, air is sucked into your body through your nose and mouth. The air becomes warm and moist, and dust and dirt are trapped by hairs and **mucus** in your nose. The air travels down your throat and into your windpipe, which branches into two tubes, called bronchi, each leading into a lung.

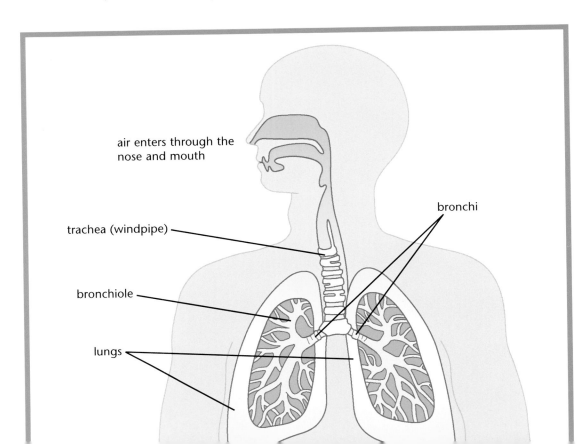

air enters through the nose and mouth

bronchi

trachea (windpipe)

bronchiole

lungs

Inside your lungs, the bronchi divide many times into smaller tubes called bronchioles. These end in millions of **microscopic** air sacs, or alveoli. The alveoli have very thin walls that are covered with tiny blood **capillaries**. Oxygen from the air in the alveoli passes into the blood inside the capillaries to be pumped around your body. At the same time as oxygen passes into the capillaries, a waste product from your blood passes into the alveoli. This waste product is **carbon dioxide** gas. When you breathe out, carbon dioxide is pushed out of your body.

How do I breathe?

Two groups of muscles work to make you breathe. One is your diaphragm, a strong sheet of muscle under your lungs. The other is the set of muscles between your ribs. When you breathe in, your diaphragm moves down and the muscles between your ribs pull your chest up and out. This makes a large space inside your chest, and your lungs swell out to fill it, sucking in air. When you breathe out, your diaphragm rises up and your ribs move down and in. The space in your chest becomes smaller and air is squeezed out of your lungs. This movement of chest muscles is very noticeable after you've just done some exercise and are breathing hard and fast.

Why do I need to eat?

You need food to survive. Food gives your body the energy it needs to keep working and moving, to build and repair body parts, and to grow. But in order to use the food you eat, your body has to **digest** it. This means breaking down your food into **chemicals** that can then be carried in your blood to wherever they are needed. The process of digestion begins when you put food into your mouth and ends when you go to the toilet. Your food travels for about 9 metres through your **digestive system** and its journey takes about 24 hours.

What happens in my mouth?

Your body's first job is to make your food small enough to swallow. Your front teeth, called incisors, bite off pieces of food and your back teeth, called premolars and molars, chew them and crush them, breaking them into bits. As your food is chewed, it is mixed up with **saliva** (spit) to make it soft and moist. Then your tongue pushes a squidgy ball of food to the back of your mouth, ready for swallowing.

What happens in my stomach?

When you swallow, food enters your oesophagus, a long tube leading into your stomach. Strong muscles squeeze it down the oesophagus, until it enters your stomach – a strong, stretchy bag which holds food and drink from one meal. The muscles in your stomach squeeze the food and mix it up with **digestive juices**, which dissolve it into a pulp.

What should I eat?

Your body needs a range of foods to keep healthy. Proteins help your body to repair itself. They are found in meat, fish, milk and cheese, and also in nuts and pulses (such as lentils).
Your body gets energy from carbohydrates, found in rice, potatoes, bread and pasta, and from fats, such as oil and butter.
Foods with **fibre** keep your digestive system working well. Muesli, fruit and vegetables have plenty of fibre.

Where does my food go next?

After your food has been in your stomach for about an hour, it is squirted into a very long coiled-up tube called the small intestine. Here it is mixed with digestive juices from a nearby **organ** called the pancreas, which break the food down into chemicals. The chemicals soak into tiny hair-like parts, called villi, on the walls of the small intestine. Inside the villi are lots of blood **capillaries**. The chemicals pass from the villi into your blood.

From your small intestine, your blood carries food chemicals to your liver – a large organ on the right of your body. Your liver sorts the chemicals into different types and sends them in the blood to the parts of your body that need them. Some chemicals are stored in your liver until they are needed.

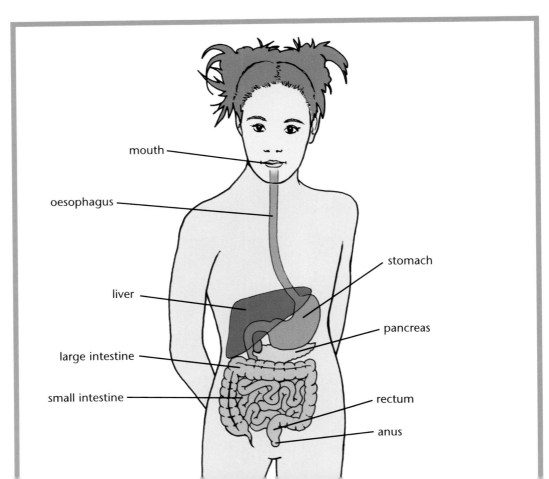

mouth

oesophagus

stomach

liver

pancreas

large intestine

small intestine

rectum

anus

What happens to the waste?

By the time your food leaves your small intestine, most of its useful chemicals have been taken out. The leftovers travel through your large intestine, which takes water out of them, turning them into solid waste. The waste is stored in a bag called the rectum, until it leaves your body through the anus.

As well as solid waste, called faeces, your body produces liquid waste, or urine. Your kidneys make urine as part of their job of cleaning your blood. Your kidneys are two small organs near the middle of your back. All the blood in your body passes through your kidneys to be cleaned about 20 times a day. The kidneys take waste chemicals and water out of your blood to form liquid urine. Urine travels down two tubes to a stretchy bag called the bladder. The urine leaves your body through a tube called the urethra.

What happens when your kidneys don't work?

People whose kidneys don't work need to have their blood cleaned every few days using a dialysis machine (see picture). If a matching kidney can be found, it is possible to have a **kidney transplant operation**.

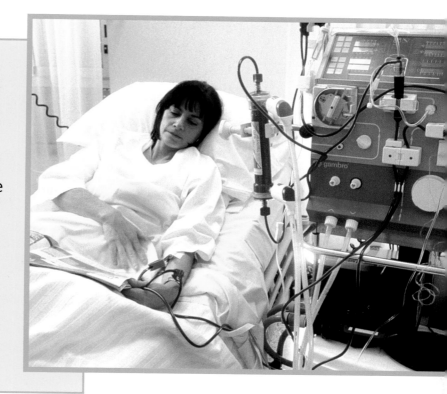

How do my senses work?

Your body has five **senses**, which tell you about your surroundings. They are sight, hearing, touch, taste and smell. Each sense has its own **organ** – eyes for sight, ears for hearing, nose for smell, tongue (and nose) for taste, and skin for touch.

How do I see things?

Whenever you see something, your eyes are collecting the light that bounces off it. Light from the object enters your eyes through a hole called a **pupil**. Then it passes through a clear disc called a lens. The lens focuses (bends) the light rays so they shine a clear, sharp image on to a screen at the back of your eyeball called the retina. The retina contains millions of light-sensitive **cells**. These cells send signals to your brain, telling it what you see.

What happens inside my eye?

This diagram shows how your eyes work. The image on the retina is upside down, but your brain turns it around.

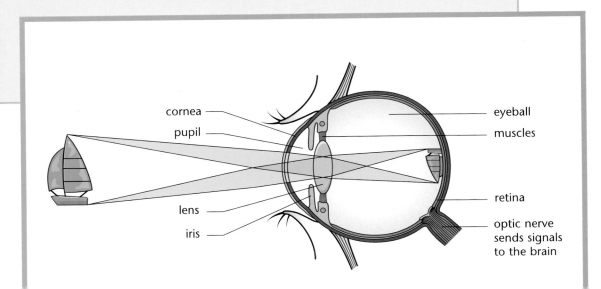

cornea
pupil
lens
iris
eyeball
muscles
retina
optic nerve sends signals to the brain

EXPERIMENT: Why do I need two eyes?

HYPOTHESIS:
Your eyes work together to produce a better image than a single eye could give.

EQUIPMENT:
A pen with a top.

EXPERIMENT STEPS:
1 Close one eye.
2 Hold up the pen in one hand and the top in the other, so they are level with your eyes.
3 With your arms slightly bent, try to put the top on the pen. Can you see if the top is in front of the pen or behind it?
4 Open both eyes and try again. Is it easier this time?
5 Write down what happened.

CONCLUSION:
It is much easier to judge distances with two eyes than one. This is because each eye gives a slightly different view. When your brain compares the two views it can work out exactly where things are. Being able to see things in this way is called 'binocular vision'.

How do I hear things?

In this diagram you can see the main parts of the ear. It stretches deep inside your head. Whenever anything makes a sound it causes **vibrations** in the air. These vibrations collect in your outer ear and travel down your ear canal until they hit a tightly stretched disc of skin called the eardrum. Then they pass along three tiny bones called the ossicles into a thick fluid inside a snail-shaped tube, called the cochlea. **Microscopic** hairs inside your cochlea pick up the vibrations and turn them into signals, which are sent along **nerves** to your brain.

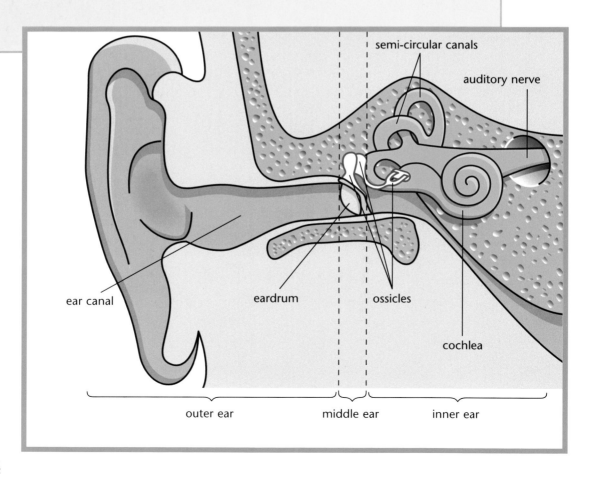

ear canal

eardrum

ossicles

semi-circular canals

auditory nerve

cochlea

outer ear

middle ear

inner ear

How do I smell things?

Smells are really tiny **particles** of a substance that float through the air. When these invisible particles from something enter you nose, you can smell it.

At the top of the inside of your nose is a patch of smell-sensitive cells. Growing from these cells are millions of tiny hairs, called cilia, which can detect different kinds of smells. When particles enter your nose, the cilia send signals along nerves to your brain. Your brain matches the signals with the smells in its memory to tell you what you are smelling. Most people can recognize up to 10,000 different smells!

How do I taste things?

The main place where you taste your food is on your tongue. It is covered with thousands of tiny pits called taste buds, and each bud is filled with sensitive 'tasting cells'. When food is dissolved with **saliva** it washes into your taste buds, and the cells send signals to your brain.

How do we sense flavours?

Your taste buds can recognize saltiness, sweetness, sourness and bitterness, but with the help of your nose, you can taste much more than this. Your tongue and nose work together to sense different flavours – that's why your food seems so tasteless when you have a blocked nose.

How do I feel things?

You feel things when they touch your skin. Just underneath the top layer of your skin are lots of different nerve endings, which can sense heat and cold, pressure and pain. The nerve endings send signals to your brain along your nerves. Then your brain uses this information to tell you how things feel.

Some parts of your skin have more nerve endings than others, which makes them extra-sensitive to touch. The most sensitive areas of your body are your lips, your fingertips and your toes.

Why is skin useful?

Skin is very useful for feeling things, but it has other uses as well. It stops your internal organs from drying out and helps to protect them from dirt and germs. Your skin also helps to keep your body at the same temperature all the time. When it's hot, your skin makes drops of sweat, which cool you down. When it's cold, tiny muscles pull the hairs on your skin upright and give you 'goose pimples' (see picture). A layer of air is trapped between the hairs and your skin, and this helps to keep you warm.

What does my brain do?

Without your brain you wouldn't be able to do anything at all. It controls everything that happens in your body. Every second of the day, your brain receives messages from different parts of your body telling it what is happening there. It also sends out signals to the different parts, giving them instructions about what to do.

How does my brain send its signals?

Your brain is connected to every part of your body through a network of tiny, thread-like **nerves**. This network is called your nervous system. Messages to and from your brain travel through your nervous system, in a split second.

Scientists are still working to find out more about the human brain. It is the most mysterious part of the amazing machine that is your body.

What does the brain look like?

The brain does not look like any other part of the body. A healthy human brain, like the one in this picture, is a highly compact

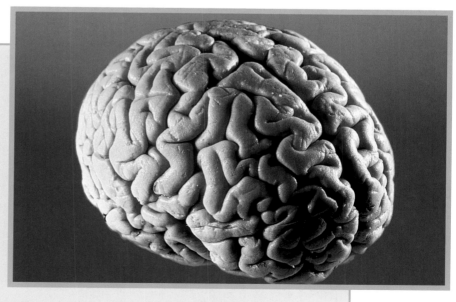

organ, made up of many folds and ridges. Sometimes it is called 'grey matter' because of its pinkish-grey colour.

People who found the answers

Galen (129–200)

Galen was a doctor in Ancient Rome who was fascinated by the human body. Romans were not allowed to **dissect** (cut up) human bodies so he dissected pigs instead. Galen worked out that the heart sends blood to different parts of the body, but he thought that blood was only sent out when it was needed.

Andreas Vesalius (1514–64)

For hundreds of years, doctors were taught Galen's ideas. But in the 1500s an Italian doctor called Vesalius began dissecting human bodies. Vesalius realized that some of Galen's ideas were wrong. He made detailed drawings of the insides of bodies – like this one showing all the **veins** in the body – and started the new subject of anatomy – the scientific study of the human body.

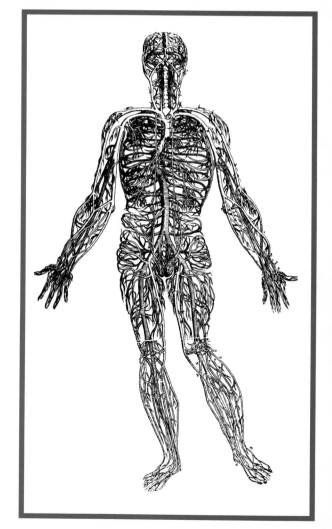

William Harvey (1578–1657)

In the 16th century, people still didn't realize that blood **circulates** around the body. But then William Harvey, an English doctor, started to do some experiments. He discovered that the heart acts like a pump, working all the time to push blood round the body.

Amazing facts

- Your body is three-quarters water. Body fluids like blood and sweat are mainly made of water, and an average person sweats about 600 ml (one pint) of water a day. This picture shows a close-up of sweat droplets on the skin surface of the back of a human hand.

- Your skin **cells** are constantly being worn away and replaced. Most house dust is made of flakes of dead skin!

- The most active muscles in your body are your eye muscles. They contract about 100,000 times a day. Lots of this movement happens while you are asleep. When you dream, your eye muscles flicker under your closed lids.

- If all the **blood vessels** in your body were joined end to end, they would measure about 95,000 kilometres. That means they could stretch more than twice round the Earth!

- An adult's heart beats around 70 times a minute, but a baby's is much faster, beating about 130 times a minute. A mouse's heart beats about 500 times a minute and an elephant's heart is incredibly slow – beating about 25 times a minute.

Glossary

artery tube that carries blood away from the heart to the rest of the body

automatic happening on its own, without you thinking about it

blood vessel tube that carries blood

bone marrow jelly-like substance inside your bones that makes new blood cells

capillary tiny tube for carrying blood. Capillaries have very thin walls.

carbon dioxide waste gas produced by the body and breathed out of the lungs

cartilage strong, flexible substance at the end of some bones

cell smallest living part of the human body. Your body is made from billions of cells.

chemical basic substance from which things are made

circulate to travel in a loop

contract (in muscles) to tighten and become shorter

digest to break down food so it can be absorbed into the blood

digestive juices liquids in the stomach and intestines that help to break down food

digestive system system of organs and tubes that food travels through to be digested

dissect to cut up something so you can study it

fibre the tough part of foods, such as the outer husks of wheat. Fibre passes through the body but is not digested.

flexible easy to bend

framework structure that provides shape and support

intestines long, coiled-up tubes that are part of the digestive system. There are two sections: the small intestine and the large intestine.

joint place where two bones meet and are joined together

kidney transplant operation operation to replace someone's damaged kidney with a healthy kidney from another person

ligaments tough, stretchy straps that link bones together

microscopic too small to be seen without a microscope

mucus slimy substance made in parts of your body, such as in your nose. Mucus protects these parts and keeps them moist.

multiply to grow in number

nerve very thin thread that sends messages between your brain and other parts of the body. A network of nerves runs through the human body.

organ major part of the body, such as the brain, heart or stomach

oxygen colourless gas found in the air. Humans and animals need to breathe in oxygen to survive.

particle extremely small part of something

pulse regular push of blood as it is pumped through your veins

pupil black hole in the middle of the coloured part of your eye. Light enters your eyes through your pupils.

relax (in muscles) to loosen and become longer

saliva liquid made in the mouth that moistens the food and starts the process of digestion; spit

sense (in the body) a way the body discovers information about its surroundings. The five senses are sight, hearing, touch, taste and smell.

swivel to turn around or rotate

vein tube that carries blood to the heart from the rest of the body

vibration rapid shaking movement back and forth

Index

More books to read

Body Matters series, Angela Royston and Louise Spilsbury (Heinemann Library 2002)
Fantastic Facts: The Body, Steven Parker (Southwater, 2000)
The Giant Book of the Body, Jackie Gaff (Aladdin, Watts, 2000)